ALONG THE WAY.

ALONG THE WAY

BY

MARY (MAPES) DODGE

> "*The air that floated by me seemed to say:*
> *'Write!'*
> *And so I did.*" . . . . KEATS.

NEW-YORK
CHARLES SCRIBNER'S SONS
1879

Press of
Francis Hart & Co.

Of the poems in this book, many are now published for the first time; others have appeared in various magazines; and a few—because they appeal to adults, and so seem to belong here—are reprinted from a volume of verses for children issued a few years ago.

CONTENTS.

PAGE.
In the Cañon 9
Once Before 12
Inverted 14
The Two Mysteries 15
The Stars 18
There 's a Wedding in the Orchard 19
What 's in a Name? 22
The Compact 24
The Difference 30
Secrets 32
Whip-poor-will 34
By the Lake 36
Heart-Oracles 38
Emerson 39
Shadow-Evidence 40
From Flower to Light 42
The Child and the Sea 46
The Umpires 48

PAGE.
Long Ago 50
My Window Ivy 52
Faith 54
Trust 56
Death in Life 58
By Moonlight 60
The Human Tie 63
An April Maiden 64
Little Words 65
Bloom 68
Snow-flakes 69
Two Summer Days 70
Over the World 72

GRASSHOPPER AND CRICKET.

The Fields:

The Grass World 75
Confidences 77
Huber 78
Fire-flies 80
Where Ignorance is Bliss 82
Reading 83

PAGE.
THE MISTAKE 84
A TALE OF THANKS 85
WRITTEN ON THE ROAD 86
THE FLOWERS 88
FULFILLMENT 91
GREETINGS 92
TO A FRIEND 93
MARCH 94
"NOW THE NOISY WINDS ARE STILL" 96
CALLING THE FLOWERS 97
A SONG OF MAY 98
BLOSSOM-SNOW 100

The Hearth:

THE CONCERT 102
ANOTHER YEAR 104
THE MINUET 107
MOTHERLESS 110
WILLIE 113
THE FOOT-PRINT IN THE SNOW 116
HOW THE NEW-YEAR CAME 118
AT THE WINDOW 122
KITTY 124
AFTER TEA 126

PAGE.
A BIRTHDAY RHYME.......127
THANKSGIVING.......130
OLD SONGS.......133
THE NIGHTLY REST.......136

IN THE CAÑON.

INTENT the conscious mountains stood,
The friendly blossoms nodded,
As through the cañon's lonely wood
We two in silence plodded.
A something owned our presence good;
The very breeze that stirred our hair
Whispered a gentle greeting;
A grand, free courtesy was there,
A welcome, from the summit bare
Down to the brook's entreating.

Stray warblers in the branches dark
Shot through the leafy passes,
While the long note of meadow-lark
Rose from the neighboring grasses;
The yellow lupines, spark on spark,

From the more open woodland way,
  Flashed through the sunlight faintly;
A wind-blown little flower, once gay,
Looked up between its petals gray
  And smiled a message saintly.

The giant ledges, red and seamed,
  The clear, blue sky, tree-fretted;
The mottled light that round us streamed,
  The brooklet, vexed and petted;
The bees that buzzed, the gnats that dreamed,
  The flitting, gauzy things of June;
    The plain, far-off, like misty ocean,
  Or, cloud-land bound, a fair lagoon,—
  They sang within us like a tune,
    They swayed us like a dream of motion.

The hours went loitering to the West,
  The shadows lengthened slowly;
The radiant snow on mountain crest
  Made all the distance holy.
Near by, the earth lay full of rest,

The sleepy foot-hills, one by one,
Dimpled their way to twilight;
And ere the perfect day was done
There came long gleams of tinted sun,
Through heaven's crimson sky-light.

Slowly crept on the listening night,
The sinking moon shone pale and slender;
We hailed the cotton-woods, in sight,
The home-roof gleaming near and tender,
Guiding our quickened steps aright.
Soon darkened all the mighty hills,
The gods were sitting there in shadow;
Lulled were the noisy woodland rills,
Silent the silvery woodland trills,—
'T was starlight over Colorado!

ONCE BEFORE.

ONCE before, this self-same air
Passed me, though I know not where.
Strange! how very like it came!
Touch and fragrance were the same;
Sound of mingled voices, too,
With a light laugh ringing through;
Some one moving—here or there—
Some one passing up the stair,
Some one calling from without,
Or a far-off childish shout;—
Simple, home-like, nothing more,
Yet it all hath been before!

No. Not to-day, nor yesterday,
Nor any day. But far away—
So long ago, so very far,
It might have been on other star.

How was it spent? and where? and when?
This life that went, yet comes again?
Was sleep its world, or death its shore?
I still the silent Past implore.
Ah! never dream had power to show
Such vexing glimpse of Long Ago.
Never a death could follow death
With love between, and home, and breath.

The spell has passed. What spendthrifts we,
Of simple, household certainty!
What golden grain we trample low
Searching for flowers that never grow!
Why, home is real, and love is real;
Nor false our honest high ideal.
Life, it is bounding, warm and strong,
And all my heart resounds with song.
It must be true, whate'er befall,
This, and the world to come are all.
And yet it puzzles me—alack!
When life that could not be, comes back!

INVERTED.

YOUTH has its griefs, its disappointments keen,
Its baffled longings and its memories;
Its anguish in a joy that once hath been;
Its languid settling in a sinful ease.

And age has pleasures, rosy, fresh and warm,
And glad beguilements and expectancies;
Its heart of boldness for a threatened storm;
Its eager launching upon sunny seas.

Youth has its losses, sad and desolate;
Its wreck of precious freight where all was sent;
Its blight of trust, its helpless heart of fate,
Its dreary knowledge of illusion spent.

For life is but a day; and, dawn or eve,
The shadows must be long when suns are low.
Old age may be surprised and loth to leave;
And youth may weary wait and long to go.

THE TWO MYSTERIES.

"In the middle of the room, in its white coffin, lay the dead child, a nephew of the poet. Near it, in a great chair, sat Walt Whitman, surrounded by little ones, and holding a beautiful little girl on his lap. She looked wonderingly at the spectacle of death, and then inquiringly into the old man's face. 'You don't know what it is, do you, my dear?' said he, and added, 'We don't either.'"

WE know not what it is, dear, this sleep so deep and still;
The folded hands, the awful calm, the cheek so pale and chill;
The lids that will not lift again, though we may call and call;
The strange, white solitude of peace that settles over all.

We know not what it means, dear, this desolate heart-pain;
This dread to take our daily way, and walk in it again;

We know not to what other sphere the loved who
leave us go,
Nor why we 're left to wonder still, nor why we do
not know.

But this we know: Our loved and dead, if they
should come this day—
Should come and ask us, "What is life?" not one
of us could say.
Life is a mystery as deep as ever death can be;
Yet oh, how dear it is to us, this life we live
and see!

Then might they say—these vanished ones—and
blessèd is the thought;
"So death is sweet to us, beloved! though we may
show you naught;
We may not to the quick reveal the mystery of
death—
Ye cannot tell us, if ye would, the mystery of
breath."

The child who enters life comes not with knowledge
or intent,
So those who enter death must go as little children
sent.
Nothing is known. But I believe that God is over-
head;
And as life is to the living, so death is to the dead.

THE STARS.

THEY wait all day unseen by us, unfelt;
  Patient they bide behind the day's full glare;
  And we who watched the dawn when they were
    there,
Thought we had seen them in the daylight melt,
While the slow sun upon the earth-line knelt.
  Because the teeming sky seemed void and bare,
  When we explored it through the dazzled air,
We had no thought that there all day they dwelt.
Yet were they over us, alive and true,
In the vast shades far up above the blue,—
The brooding shades beyond our daylight ken—
  Serene and patient in their conscious light,
Ready to sparkle for our joy again,—
  The eternal jewels of the short-lived night.

THERE 'S A WEDDING IN THE ORCHARD.

THERE 's a wedding in the orchard, dear,
  I know it by the flowers;
They 're wreathed on every bough and branch,
  Or falling down in showers.

The air is in a mist, I think,
  And scarce knows which to be—
Whether all fragrance, clinging close,
  Or bird-song, wild and free.

And countless wedding-jewels shine,
  And golden gifts of grace;
I never saw such wealth of sun
  In any shady place.

It seemed I heard the fluttering robes
  Of maidens clad in white,

The clasping of a thousand hands
  In tenderest delight;

While whispers ran among the boughs
  Of promises and praise;
And playful, loving messages
  Sped through the leaf-lit ways.

Then were there swayings to and fro;
  The weeds a-tiptoe rose;
And sang the breeze a sudden song
  That sank to sudden close;

And just beyond the wreathèd aisles
  That end against the blue,
The raiment of the wedding-choir
  And priest came shining through.

And though I saw no wedding-guest,
  Nor groom, nor gentle bride,
I know that holy things were asked,
  And holy love replied.

Soon will the lengthening shadows move
  Unwillingly away,
Like friends who linger with adieux
  Yet are not bid to stay.

I follow where the blue-bird leads,
  And hear its soft "good-night,"
Still thinking of the wedding-scene
  And aisles of flowery light.

"WHAT 'S IN A NAME."

ONCE on a time, where jewels flashed
And rose-hid fountains softly plashed,
And all the air was sweet and bright
With music, mirth and deft delight—
A courtly dame drew, smiling, near
  A poet, greatest of his time,
And chirped a question in his ear
  With voice like silver bells in chime:
"Good Master Shakespeare, I would know
  The name thy lady bore, in sooth,
Ere thine? Nay, little while ago
  It was, for still we see her youth.
Some high-born name, I trow, and yet
Though I have heard it, I forget."
        Then answered he,
        With dignity,
  Yet blithely, as the hour was gay:
        "Ann Hathaway."

"And good, sweet sir," the dame pursued,
Too fair and winsome to be rude—
"'T is hinted here, and whispered there,
By doughty knights and ladies fair,
That—that—well, that her loyal lord
  Doth e'en obey her slightest will.
Now, my good spouse, I pledge my word,
  Though loving well, doth heed me ill.
Her witchery I pray thee tell,"
  She pleaded, with a pretty frown,
"I fain would know what mighty spell
  Can bring a haughty husband down."
Flushing, she raised her eager face
To his, with merry, plaintive grace.
        Then answered he,
        With dignity,
  Yet blithely, as the hour was gay:
        "Fair lady, I can only say,
        Ann hath a way."

THE COMPACT.

It was a little boy who lived in Philadelphia town,
And a very kind old gentleman, whose name was
    Mr. Brown.
It happened that the self-same day they visited the
    Fair,
And, hand in hand, they walked about, a happy,
    friendly pair.

The little boy looked right and left with eager, won-
    dering eyes,
The other gazed more steadily, for he was old and
    wise;
But soon he caught the small boy's way of feeling
    glad and bright;
And the boy no longer aimlessly looked to the left
    and right.

"I like you, Mr. Brown," he said. "You make me understand."

"I like *you*, too," thought Mr. Brown, and pressed the little hand.

And so they walked together, and saw the mighty show,

While music, light, and brilliant hues set all the crowd aglow.

Then, suddenly, a shadow fell upon the old man's face;

He fixed his eyes right wistfully upon the wondrous place.

"Ah, me! ah, me!" he muttered, as to himself, nor smiled

At the merry look of questioning that came upon the child.

"My boy, a hundred years from now, another mighty Fair

Will crown the new Centennial; but we shall not be there.

Not one of all this eager crowd" (and here he drew
a sigh)
"Will be living on the earth that day—not even you
and I.

"The years will bring discoveries, inventions, manners new,
And nations yet unborn may shame the things that
here we view.
I own I 'd like to see it all, the next Centennial
Fair,
With the Stars and Stripes that day, as now, flung
gayly to the air.

"I 'd like to see the world grown wiser, better, too,
my lad
(Though I 'm not one of those who think this world
is wholly bad).
I 'd like to see the country shine with nobler, holier
grace,
And the Church of Christ triumphant in the manners
of a race.

"It 's useless to regret, I know; our life is but a
span.
We 'll all be gone before that day; yes, all, my little
man."
Then Brown wiped off his spectacles, and gave a
quiet cough;
But the little boy said: "Never mind, it 's such a
long way off."

"Yes, long for you, perhaps, my boy; but *my* life 's
nearly spent.
Yet, if I knew just how the world would grow, I 'd
be content."
The little boy stopped short, with: "Here are
benches, let 's sit down.
I 'll tell you what I 'll do for you, with pleasure,
Mr. Brown.

"When I get big, I 'll notice sharp just what the
people do,
And how they live, how good they are—I 'll watch
them just for you.

And then I 'll tell some little boy (not born yet) he
must keep
A sharp lookout, and, don't you see? in time he 'll
learn a heap.

"Well, when I 'm old, I 'll say to him what you
have said to-day:
'My boy, my time is nearly spent; I 'll soon be
going away;
I can't see the Centennial that 's coming soon, I
know;
But you will see it, certainly, before you have to go.

"'Now, I 'm going,' I 'll say, 'to Heaven; and
when you come there, too,
You can tell me all about the show, and what you
saw there new,
And how the people looked and did in Philadelphia
town,
For I want to tell a friend of mine up there, named
Mr. Brown.'"

He ceased. The old man stared, then smiled and
stroked the sunny head.
"Thank you, my boy, I 'll count on you." And
that was all they said.
Then, quite content and glad again, the mighty show
they scanned,—
The old man and the little boy,—still walking hand
in hand.

THE DIFFERENCE.

I.

YESTERDAY, the wind it moaned,
The sleet drove fast, the forest groaned,
Yet within all was bright—
My heart, it was light;
The birdies were flinging
Their wealth to my singing;
The glad summer sky
It shone in his eye—
For Robin was here,
Robin, my dear!
Ah, little cared I for the gloom of the weather,
So Robin and I could but whisper together.

II.

To-day, I coldly scan it o'er,
This flood of sun on the silent floor,
        As it glitters and trembles,
        And vainly dissembles.
        The birdies outside,
        They mock and deride;
        And the sky looks me through
        With its cold eye of blue;
        For Robin is gone—
        Robin, my own!
Ah, what does it matter how sparkling the weather,
If Robin and I cannot ramble together?

SECRETS.

I 'D like to be a daisy
In the clover,
That I might look up bravely
At my lover.

I 'd bid the willing breezes
Bend me sweet,
That I might, as he passed me,
Touch his feet;

I 'd let the dew so quickly
Start and glisten,
That, thinking I had called him,
He would listen.

Yet would he listen vainly—
Happy me!
No bee could find my secret;
How could he?

If ever of the clover
Couch he made,
I 'd softly kiss his eyelids
In the shade.

Then would I breathe sweet incense
All for him,
And fill with perfect bloom
The twilight dim.

What should I do, I wonder,
When he went?
Why, I would—like a daisy—
Be content.

Alack! to live so bravely,
Peace o'erladen,
Has ne'er been granted yet
To simple maiden.

WHIP-POOR-WILL.

THE Western sky blazed through the trees,
  And in the East the dove-light shone;
Low fields of clover to the breeze
  Gave out a fragrant monotone;
While sharp-voiced, whirring things beyond
  Sent a faint treble through the air,
And discords of the hidden pond
  Pulsed like an anthem, deep and rare.
Yet all the twilight range seemed still,
  The tumult was so subtle-sweet;
  When forth it burst,—clear, slow, complete,
The evening call of
                "Whip-poor-will!"

The yarrow, crowding by the hedge,
  Stirred not its specked, uncertain white;
The locust on the upland's edge
  Stood tranced against the blaze of light;
For now the throbbing air was mute,
  Since that wild note had pierced it through,—
That call so clear, so resolute,
  So tender, dominant and true.
When suddenly, across the hill,—
  Long, low and sweet, with dreamy fall,
  Yet true and mellow, call for call,
Elate, and with a human thrill,—
Came the far answer:
                    "Whip-poor-will!"

BY THE LAKE.

I LISTEN to the plashing of the lake,—
  The tideless tide that silvers all its edge,
  And stirs, yet rouses not, the sleepy sedge,—
While the glad, busy sky is wide awake,
And coves along the shore its fleeting shadows take.

I listen to the plashing, clear and faint;
  Now sharp against the stones that slide it back,
  Now soft and nestling in a mossy track,
Or rocking in an eager, homeless plaint,
Or stifled in the ooze, whose yielding is restraint.

Nature's deep lessons come in silences,
  Or sounds that fall like silence on our sense;
  And so this plashing seeks my soul's pretense,
And bids it say what its fulfillment is,
And bares to searching light its fond alliances.

I cannot fathom all my soul doth hide,
  Nor sound the centres that the waves conceal;
  Yet in a dim, half-yearning way I feel
The urging of the low, insistent tide,—
Till the plashing seems like sobbing, and the sky
    grows cold and wide.

HEART-ORACLES.

By the motes do we know where the sunbeam is
slanting;
Through the hindering stones speaks the soul of
the brook;
Past the rustle of leaves we press in to the stillness;
Through darkness and void to the Pleiads we look;
One bird-note at dawn with the night-silence o'er us,
Begins all the morning's munificent chorus.

Through sorrow come glimpses of infinite gladness;
Through grand discontent mounts the spirit of
youth;
Loneliness foldeth a wonderful loving;
The breakers of Doubt lead the great tide of
Truth;
And dread and grief-haunted the shadowy portal
That shuts from our vision the splendor immortal.

EMERSON.

We took it to the woods, we two,
  The book well worn and brown,
To read his words where stirring leaves
  Rained their soft shadows down.

Yet as we sat and breathed the scene,
  We opened not a page;
Enough that he was with us there,
  Our silent, friendly sage!

His fresh "Rhodora" bloomed again;
  His "Humble-bee" buzzed near;
And oh, the "Wood-notes" beautiful
  He taught our souls to hear.

So our unopened book was read;
  And so, in restful mood,
We and our poet, arm in arm,
  Went sauntering through the wood.

SHADOW-EVIDENCE.

I.

SWIFT o'er the sunny grass,
I saw a shadow pass
With subtle charm;
So quick, so full of life,
With thrilling joy so rife,
I started lest, unknown,
My step—ere it was flown—
Had done it harm.

II.

Why look up to the blue?
The bird was gone, I knew,
Far out of sight.
Steady and keen of wing,
The slight, impassioned thing,

Intent on a goal unknown,
Had held its course alone
In silent flight.

III.

Dear little bird, and fleet,
Flinging down at my feet
Shadow for song:
More sure am I of thee—
Unseen, unheard by me—
Than of some things felt and known,
And guarded as my own,
All my life long.

FROM FLOWER TO LIGHT.

In sorrow I tended my garden,
  As the colors, day by day,
Faded and changed in the heedless air,
  And passed with the summer away.

While they gladdened my beautiful garden,
  Where the dews and the sunlight abide,
And crept up the wall to my window,
  Or hid, as the sweetest will hide;

While they lavished their splendor before me,
  Not a flower had I heart to cull—
Till the heaven-lit flames of the latest
  Went out, and my garden was dull.

O cruel the death of the blossoms,
  And cruel the words that were said:
"Next Spring shall the earth be re-gladdened,
  The living shall bloom from the dead."

Not for me would the blooming be, ever,
  For my love, O my love! could not stay.
Hand in hand we had bent o'er their brightness,
  And now he was passing away.

The heart-breaking flowers of next summer,
  They will look at me, dreary and wan,
Or mock me, and taunt me, and madden—
  O God, that the years should roll on!

So I felt; and I would not look skyward,
  Nor earthward, but only at him—
At him with his clear dying vision,
  Who saw not the earth growing dim.

At him, till alone in the garden
  I stood with the husks of the flowers;

Alone, and the pitiless Autumn
  Sent dead leaves about me, in showers.

"Look up!" he had whispered in parting;
  "Look up!" said a voice to me then,—
And lo! the lost hues of my garden
  Above me were glowing again!

Near by, in the wide-spreading maples;
  Far-off, in the mist of the wood;
Around and above me they gathered,
  And lit all the place where I stood.

My purples, my rose-tints and yellows,
  My crimsons that gladdened his sight,
My glorious hues of the garden
  Were living in sunnier height!

Were living! were living! I knew it!
  And the comfort that came to me so,
Endured when the forest was naked
  And the grass covered over with snow.

For again I looked up and beheld them,
  The souls of the flowers he had blest;
I saw them in glory transfigured
  Far off in the wonderful West.

Contented, at last, I beheld them—
  My colors immortal and bright—
When the gates of the sunset, slow-folding,
  Shut them out from my passionate sight.

THE CHILD AND THE SEA.

ONE Summer day, when birds flew high,
  I saw a child step into the sea;
It glowed, and sparkled at her touch,
  And softly plashed about her knee.
It held her lightly with its strength,
  It kissed and kissed her silken hair;
It swayed with tenderness to know
  A little child was in its care.

She, gleeful, dipped her pretty arms,
  And caught the sparkles in her hands;
I heard her laughter, as she soon
  Came skipping up the sunny sands.
"Is this the cruel sea?" I thought,
  "The merciless, the awful sea?"—
Now hear the answer soft and true,
  That rippled over the beach to me:

"Shall not the sea, in the sun, be glad
  When a child doth come to play?
Had it been in the storm-time, what could I,
  The sea, but bear her away—
Bear her away on my foaming crest,
  Toss her and hurry her to her rest?

"Be it life or death, God ruleth me;
  And he loveth every soul;
I've an earthly shore and a heavenly shore,
  And toward them both I roll;
Shining and beautiful, both, are they,—
  And a little child will go God's way."

THE UMPIRES.

I.

We chose our blossoms, sitting on the grass;
  His, Marguerites, with sunny, winsome faces,
  Mine the bright clover, with its statelier graces.
"Let these decide the argument, my lass;
We 'll watch," said he, "the light-winged breezes pass
  And note which first the earliest whiff displaces;
  If it be daisy, yours the sore disgrace is,
And be it clover, then I yield, alas!"
The lightsome quarrel was but half in jest;
I would go homeward; he would sit and rest—
The foolish cousin whom I would not wed.
Smiling we waited; not a word we said.
In earnest he, and I quite debonair—
But oh, the stillness of that summer air!

II.

So still it was—so still with quiet heat,
 The blossom lately from the brooklet quaffing
 Ceased its brisk dipping and sly telegraphing,
And scorned the blossom opposite to greet.
The very grass stood breathless at our feet;
 When, suddenly, our weighty silence chaffing,
 The leaves around broke out in muffled laughing,
And something stirred the fickle Marguerite!
 "Your flower!" I cried.—"Ah, now it bends quite over!"
 "Oho!" he answered—"see your nodding clover!"
 In truth, those silly blossoms fluttered so,
 I really knew not if to stay or go.—
 And so it happened that the twilight found me
 Still resting there,—and Charlie's arm around me.

LONG AGO.

Still the rock is in the forest,
 With the branches overhead,
And the linden-tree, low-bending
 By the sumac, flaming red.
In and out among the shadows
 Glides the self-same woodland stream;
Still the bright-eyed squirrels listen,
 And the beetles idly dream.

Do the squirrels hear a foot-fall,
 Or the beetles flash their green
For a hand that parts the branches,
 Letting sun-light in between?
Does the brook, with rippling lightness,
 Catch two shadows—his and mine—
Give them to its circling eddies
 With a murmuring divine?

Do the lichens, gray and clinging,
  Hear a promise whispered there,
While the ferns look up and listen,
  Laughing through the maiden-hair?
Do the birds that fill the distance,
  Or the glints of summer blue,
Try to sing and shine love's gladness
  As of old they used to do?

Ah, for comfort of all rovers,
  Such as I, in stranger clime;
Sure as sunlight, new-made lovers
  Roam to-day the summer's prime.
Heaven spare the fields their brightness!
  Spare the brook its sparkling flow!
Light the woods with holy shadows
  As it lit them long ago!

MY WINDOW-IVY.

OVER my window the ivy climbs,
  Its roots are in homely jars;
But all the day it looks at the sun,
  And at night looks out at the stars.

The dust of the room may dim its green,
  But I call to the breezy air:
"Come in, come in, good friend of mine!
  And make my window fair."

So the ivy thrives from morn to morn,
  Its leaves all turned to the light;
And it gladdens my soul with its tender green,
  And teaches me day and night.

What though my lot is in lowly place,
  And my spirit behind the bars;
All the long day I may look at the sun,
  And at night look out at the stars.

What though the dust of earth would dim,
  There 's a glorious outer air
That will sweep through my soul if I let it in,
  And make it fresh and fair.

Dear God! let me grow from day to day,
  Clinging and sunny and bright!
Though planted in shade, Thy window is near,
  And my leaves may turn to the light.

FAITH.

THE wind drove the moon
  To a sky-built cave,
And closed it up
  As it were her grave.
The cave threw wide
  A silver portal —
And forth she came,
  Serene, immortal!

He piled black clouds
  In angry might,
Till lost in gloom
  Was all her light.
The clouds a moment
  Held her under;
Then, glorified,
  They burst asunder!

The wind, that night,
  Bemoaned and whistled
Till all the forest
  Stirred and bristled;
While moonbeams stole
  To tear-wet pillows,
And found their way
  Through grave-yard willows.

TRUST.

THOUGH tangled hard life's knot may be,
And wearily we rue it,
The silent touch of Father Time
Some day will sure undo it.
Then, darling, wait;
Nothing is late
In the light that shines forever.

We faint at heart, a friend is gone;
We chafe at the world's harsh drilling;
We tremble at sorrows on every side,
At the myriad ways of killing.
Yet, say we all,
If a sparrow fall,
The Lord keepeth count forever.

He keepeth count. We come, we go,
We speculate, toil and falter:
But the measure to each of weal or woe,
God only can give or alter.

He sendeth light,
He sendeth night,
And change goes on forever.

Why not take life with cheerful trust,
With faith in the strength of weakness?
The slenderest daisy rears its head
With courage, yet with meekness.
A sunny face
Hath holy grace,
To woo the Sun forever.

Forever and ever, my darling, yes—
Goodness and love are undying;
Only the troubles and cares of earth
Are winged from the first for flying.
Our way we plow
In the furrow "now";
But after the tilling and growing, the sheaf;
Soil for the root, but the sun for the leaf,—
And God keepeth watch forever.

DEATH IN LIFE.

SHE sitteth there a mourner,
  With her dead before her eyes;
Flushed with the hues of life is he
  And quick are his replies.
Often his warm hand touches hers;
  Brightly his glances fall;
And yet, in this wide world, is she
  The loneliest of all.

Some mourners feel their dead return
  In dreams, or thoughts at even;
Ah, well for them their best-beloved
  Are faithful still in heaven!
But woe to her whose best-beloved,
  Though dead, still lingers near;
So far away when by her side,
  He cannot see nor hear.

With heart intent, he comes, he goes
  In busy ways of life.
His gains and chances counteth he;
  His hours with joy are rife.
Careless he greets her day by day,
  Nor thinks of words once said.—
Oh, would that love could live again,
  Or her heart give up its dead!

BY MOONLIGHT.

Out of the depths above shone forth
  A beautiful, radiant, peerless light;
Paling the stars near by, she ruled
  Queen of the breathless, listening night.

Four of us glided along in the boat,—
  Rhoda and Etta, Harry and I,—
Cheerily watching the glory that streamed
  Across the sea from the bending sky.

Etta spoke first, and her voice seemed far:
  "The sparkling line, however we turn,
Comes straight to me!" But I claimed it, too,
  I at the bow, and she at the stern.

We laughed, insisting; then Rhoda, between: —
  "Absurd! for it comes to me, not you—
A beautiful, silvery ribbon of light,
  Crinkling and shining across the blue."

Then Harry, the rower: "By all that 's bright
  It flashes its course direct to me!"
Thus merry, intent and apart we sat,
  Claiming the splendor that crossed the sea

Till Rhoda, the fairy, proposed a plan
  (A friskier sailor was never afloat);
And then, with many a laugh and start,
  We all changed seats in the rocking boat.

O human vision, how blind it is!
  'T was plain, at last, that our partial sight
Had made the glory that shone for all
  To each seem a narrow pathway bright.

Shining, arose on the breast of the sea,
  A lesson in love, a thought of grace:

Learn thou to look for the Heavenly light
Not alone from thine own, but thy neighbor's place.

Four of us glided home in the boat,
Rhoda and Etta, Harry and I,
Thoughtfully watching the glory that streamed
Over the sea from the silent sky.

THE HUMAN TIE.

"*As if life were not sacred, too.*"—GEORGE ELIOT.

"SPEAK tenderly! For he is dead," we say;
  "With gracious hand smooth all his roughened past,
  And fullest measure of reward forecast,
Forgetting naught that gloried his brief day."
Yet of the brother, who, along our way,
  Prone with his burdens, heart-worn in the strife,
  Totters before us—how we search his life,
Censure, and sternly punish, while we may.
Oh, weary are the paths of Earth, and hard!
And living hearts alone are ours to guard.
At least, begrudge not to the sore distraught
The reverent silence of our pitying thought.
Life, too, is sacred; and he best forgives
Who says: "He errs, but—tenderly! He lives."

AN APRIL MAIDEN.

"WERE you ever heavy-hearted, little May?"
She tossed her sunny head,
As right merrily she said:
"Heavy-hearted? No, not I;
Yet a little makes me cry,
And a little less than half
Makes me laugh—
My mother often calls me 'April Day.'"

"Were you ever very happy, little May?"
Again she shook her head:
"I do not know," she said;
"Very happy? Who is so?
Not a single soul, you know.
Mother often tells me this
With a kiss:—
Our life, she says, is like an April day."

LITTLE WORDS.

How wise he is! He can talk in Greek!
There is n't a language he cannot speak.
The very measure the Psalmist sung
He carries at will on the tip of his tongue.
When he argues in English, why, every word
Is almost the biggest that ever you heard!
That is, when he talks with Papa it 's so—
With me it 's another affair, you know.

Little one-syllable words, you see,
Are all he is willing to waste upon me;
So he calls me his rose, his bird, his pet,
And says it quite often, lest I should forget;

While his wonderful verbs grow meagre and small;
You 'd think he had ne'er opened Webster at all.
It 's only: "Ah, do you?" or "Will you, my dove?"
Or else it 's: "I love," "I love," and "I love."

And when we walk out in the starry night,
Though he knows the Zodiac's rounded height,
With its Gemini, Scorpio, Leo, and all,
Its nebulæ, planets, and satellites small,
And though, in a flash, he could turn his proud eye on
The Dipper, and Crown, and the Belt of Orion;—
Not once does he mention the wonders above,
But just whispers softly: "My own!" and "I love!"

Whenever they tease me—the girls and boys—
With: "Mrs. Professor," or "classical joys;"
Or ask if his passion he deigns to speak
In Hebrew, or Sanscrit or simple Greek;—
I try to summon a look of steel,
And hide the joy that I really feel.
For they 'd laugh still more if they knew the truth
How meek a professor can be, forsooth!

Though well I know, in the days to come
Great thoughts shall preside in our happy home;
And to hold forever his loving looks
I must bend my head over musty books,
And be as learned as ever I can
To do full justice to such a man,—
The future is bright, for, like song of birds,
My soul is filled with his little words.

BLOOM.

THE sudden sun shone through the pane
  And lighted both their faces—
A prettier sight just after rain
  Ne'er fell in pleasant places:

Two girls. One held a vase of glass,
  And one a bulb unsightly,
Ragged and soiled. And this the lass
  Upon the vase laid lightly.

"What lovely flowers we 'll have," said they,
  "After it starts a-growing!"
The sun, delighted, slipped away
  And down the west went glowing.

SNOW-FLAKES.

Whenever a snow-flake leaves the sky,
It turns and turns to say "Good-bye!
Good-bye, dear cloud, so cool and gray!"
Then lightly travels on its way.

And when a snow-flake finds a tree,
"Good-day!" it says—"Good-day to thee!
Thou art so bare and lonely, dear,
I 'll rest, and call my comrades here."

But when a snow-flake, brave and meek,
Lights on a rosy maiden's cheek,
It starts—"How warm and soft the day!
'T is summer!"—and it melts away.

TWO SUMMER DAYS.

"June 17th.

"*It was only a little bunch of clover-blossoms gathered for her, near a way-side station, soon after our parties were introduced on the East-bound train. But how much it meant! That was just one year ago to-day,—and now we are going back together!*"—From his Letter.

A year ago this day, my girl,
  The clover told a thing to you,
Amid the stir and noisy whirl
  Of wheels, as toward his home we flew;
And now you know how fond and true
The thing the clover said to you.

With modest mirth and girlish grace,
  You took the gift and lightly smiled;
You pressed it softly to your face,
  (What wonder that the flower grew wild!)
And now, in thought, again we trace,
The clover bloom, the girlish grace.

Over the self-same road again
  You journey,—yours the homeward way;
And bright upon that Western plain
  The nodding clover smiles to-day;
And still, though not in lightsome play,
It has a blessed thing to say.

Still waves the clover in the sun,
  And whispers near the whirring track:
"Two lives are floating into one,
  Two travellers are speeding back.
God bless them both till Heaven is won,
And bless the love in bloom begun!"

OVER THE WORLD.

THERE is a time between our night and day,
A space between this world and the unknown,
Where none may enter as we stand alone
Save the one other single soul that may;
Then is all perfect if the two but stay.
It is the time when, the home-evening flown,
And "good-nights" sped in happy household tone,
We look out from the casement ere we pray.
Into the world of darkness deep and far
We gaze—each depth with its own deepest star,
That brightens as we turn, nor yet recedes
When we would search it with our sorest needs,—
O holy living-ground from heaven won!
O time beyond the night when day is done!

GRASSHOPPER AND CRICKET.

"*One to the fields, the other to the hearth.*"
LEIGH HUNT.

THE GRASS-WORLD.

OH, life is rife in the heart of the year,
  When midsummer suns sail high:
And under the shadow of spike and spear,
  In the depth of the daisy sky,
There's a life unknown to the careless glance;
And under the stillness an airy prance,
  And slender, jointed things astir,
  And gossamer wings in a sunny whir,—
And a world of work and dance.

Soft in its throbbing, the conscious green
  Demurely answers the breeze;
While down in its tangle, in riotous sheen,
  The hoppers are bending their knees:

And only a beetle, or lumbering ant,
As he pushes a feathery spray aslant,—
  Or the sudden dip of a foraging bird,
  With its vibrant trail of the clover stirred,
Discovers the secret haunt.

Ah, the grass-world dies in the autumn days,
  When, studded with sheaf and stack,
The fields lie browning in sullen haze,
  And creak in the farmer's track.
Hushed is the tumult the daisies knew,
The hidden sport of the supple crew;
  And lonely and dazed in the glare of day,
  The stiff-kneed hoppers refuse to play
In the stubble that mocks the blue.
  For all things feel that the time is drear
  When life runs low in the heart of the year.

CONFIDENCES.

I WATCHED a butterfly on the wing;
I saw him alight on a sunny spray.
  His pinions quivered;
  The blossom shivered;
I know he whispered some startling thing.
  But why so bold,
  Or what he told,
While poising there on the sunny spray,
I never have learned to this blessèd day.

I watched a brave young cavalier;
I saw him steal to a maiden gay.
  Swift words he muttered;
  The maiden fluttered;
I know his whisper she flushed to hear.
  But why so bold,
  Or what he told,
While bending there by the maiden gay,
She never has owned to this blessèd day.

HUBER.

A BLIND man under the linden trees,
Listening hour by hour.
The tall, white clover is tapping his knees—
Impatient, eager flower!
"See! See!
He comes. My bee!
Good friend, you know who is come to me!"—
And now the blind man sees.

He sees!
Oh, wonderful eyes of the sense and soul,
Eyes that, seeing the least so well,
Must see the whole!
And, bees,—
With your booms and buzzings that daze the air,
Your droning cadence with mystic swell,
Your pilot flights and reckonings rare,
And the hoards you drew
From bloom and dew,—

Do you know of the hoard you have stored for
him
Who works and waits in the darkness dim?
From fields where our easy vision fails
In the light where our sunniest sunlight pales,
You carry your store
Of Nature's lore.
Your lives and secrets his soul doth scan,
Giving him glimpse of the Infinite Plan.
Wonderful, wonderful bees,—
For Huber sees!

FIRE-FLIES.

SEE the air filling near by and afar,—
A shadowy host—how brilliant they are!

Silently flitting, spark upon spark,
Gemming the willows out in the dark;

Waking the night in a twinkling surprise,
Making the star-light pale where they rise;

Snowing soft fire-flakes into the grass,
Lighting the face of each daisy they pass;

Startling the darkness, over and over,
Where the sly pimpernel kisses the clover;

Piercing the duskiest heights of the pines;
Drowsily poised on the low-swinging vines;

Suddenly shifting their tapers around,
Now on the fences, and now on the ground,

Now in the bushes and tree-tops, and then
Pitching them far into darkness again;

There like a shooting-star, slowly on wing,
Here like the flash of a dowager's ring;

Setting the dark, croaking hollows a-gleam,
Spangling the gloom of the ghoul-haunted stream;

They pulse and they sparkle in shadowy play,
Like a night fallen down with its stars all astray;

They pulse and they flicker, they kindle afar,
A vanishing host,—but how brilliant they are!

WHERE IGNORANCE IS BLISS.

Two little sorrel blossoms, pale and slender,
  Lean to each other in the cool, tall grass;
The crowding spears with gallant air and tender,
Shield them completely from the sun's fierce splendor,
  Till harmlessly an angry wind might pass.
And I stand smiling with a sudden whim:
  "The little innocents! Now am I sure
      They think them in a forest grand and dim,
      The mighty grass coëval with their birth,—
Shut from the world, from every ill secure,
  And where their thicket ends, there ends the earth!"

READING.

ONE day in the bloom of a violet
  I found a simple word;
And my heart went softly humming it,
  Till the violet must have heard.

And deep in the depth of a crimson rose
  A writing showed so plain,
I scanned it over in veriest joy
  To the patter of summer rain.

And then from the grateful mignonette
  I read—ah, such a thing!
That the glad tears fell on it like dew,
  And my soul was ready to sing.

A few little words! Before that day
  I never had taken heed;
But, oh, how I blessed the love that came—
  The love that taught me to read!

THE MISTAKE.

Little Rosy Redcheek said unto a clover:
"Flower, why were you made?
I was made for mother,
She has n't any other,
But you were made for no one, I'm afraid."

Then the clover softly unto Redcheek whispered:
"Pluck me, ere you go."
Redcheek, little dreaming,
Pulled, and ran off screaming,
"Oh, naughty, naughty flower to sting me so!"

"Foolish one!" the startled bee buzzed crossly,
"Foolish not to see
That I make my honey,
While the day is sunny;
That the pretty little clover lives for me."

A TALE OF THANKS.

DEAR rose! that tinted my baby's cheek,
I praise thee more than words can speak;
And gentian! darling of autumn skies,
I thank thee for her soft blue eyes;
Oh, summer brook! from thy ripples bright
Her smiles do borrow their dancing light;
And satin cell of the chestnut burr,
What lustre of hair thou hast lent to her!
Oh, lithe young sapling, growing apace,
Honor to thee for her supple grace;
And living sunshine, well I know
Thou gavest her warm young heart its glow.
In truth, not a charm of earth or sky
But comes for my girl to pattern by;
And truly I thank you, every one,
For the sweetest lassie the sun shines on!

WRITTEN ON THE ROAD.

(MAY, 1879.)

OUT in the sunshine fair and free,
Flecked by the blossoming, re-born tree,
Bathed in the pale, pure light of Spring,
While men look up, and the glad birds sing,—
There, dear friend, let thy reck'ning be,
So let thy birthdays come to thee!

Firm as the tall, brave trunks around;
Full of life as the flower-full ground;
Free as the boughs that sweep the blue;
Bright as the violet's sudden hue;—
So let thy life-long reck'ning be,
So let thy birthdays come to thee!

It was cool and gray in the twilight morn—
A prophecy sweetest—when thou wast born;
And if daylight gathered a cloud or two
That floated beside thee when life was new,

Thy noon will be sunny and clear, I know,
And holy and peaceful thine evening glow—
  For good and true shall thy reck'ning be
  Till all thy birthdays are come to thee.

UNISON.

Over us the wild, cool Night
  Spread her dark tresses heavy with quick gems,
Till in the twinkling blackness, lithe and light,
  We felt like wood-flowers swung on hidden stems.

THE FLOWERS.

THEY 'RE coming! they 're coming!
  'T is writ on the air,
In incense and harmony
  Breathed everywhere!
Winds murmur no longer
  Their woe to the pines—
But spiders are spinning
  Their gossamer lines.
Blue-birds are darting
  The branches among,
Wild with a pleasure
  Only half sung.
Willows are greening
  Down by the brook;
Insects are stirring
  In forest and nook;

Sunlight is bringing
  Buttercups sweet—
Hear the grass whisper
  Under our feet!
Telling of daisies,
  Telling of clover,
Telling of beauty
  All the world over.

They 're coming! They 're coming!
  The beautiful throng,
To soothe us and cheer us
  The whole summer long.
By brook, and in meadow,
  Woodland and glade,
Through moonlight and star-light
  Sunshine and shade,
They 're creeping, they 're springing,
  They 're climbing the hill,
They 're twining and clinging—
  Though underground still;

The blue-birds have called them,—
  The roses and all;
They have heard, and already
  They answer the call!

O Snow-white and Purple,
  Pink, Yellow and Blue!
Lie close to their hearts
  Till the day they come through
O Spirit of Beauty!
  Spirit of Grace!
Still bide ye above them
  Watching the place.
Fragrance and loveliness
  Still hover near,
Soon shall your hosts
  In their glory appear.
Surely the Spring-time
  Is crowning its hours—
They 're coming! They 're coming—
  The beautiful flowers!

FULFILLMENT.

WAKING in May, the peach-tree thought:
" Idle and bare and weaving naught!
Here have I slept the winter through—
I with my Master's work to do!"

Started the buds. The blossoms came,
Till all the branches were a-flame.
She rocked the birds, and wove the green,
A busy tree as ever was seen.

Busy and blithe, she drank the dew;
She caught the sunbeams gliding through;
She drew her wealth from sky and soil,
And rustled gayly in her toil.

Now see the peach-tree's drooping head,
With all her fruit a-blushing red!
Knowing her Master's work is done,
She meekly resteth in the sun.

GREETINGS.

"Good day!" cried one who drove to West,
"Good day!" the other, Eastward bound;—
Strong, hearty voices both, that rang
Above their wagons' rattling sound.
And I, within my snug home nest,
"Good day! good day!" still softly sang.
I saw them not, yet well I knew
How much a cheery word can do,
How braced those hearts that on their way
Speed, each to each, a brave "good day!"

TO A FRIEND.

I ROAMED with thee the mountain-side,
And, with thee, watched the shadows fall;
The sun went down, but night flung wide
A glory mightier than all.

And we have walked the fields, we twain,
And said: "How fair the distance shows!
How far they blend—the sky and plain!
How holy-bright the twilight glows!"

And, hill or plain, thy soul was high,—
High as the peaks that lift to God;
And not more true than thee the sky
That shone, as on our way we trod.

. MARCH.

Ho! warrior month, my Martius, hail!
    With battling breeze and clarion call
Thou rushest over hill and vale.
Before thee kneels the glowing year;
Behind, thy glittering hosts appear.
    To rescue earth from icy thrall
    Thou comest, bravest month of all!

Dear, bustling March, my *Frühling* come!
    First month to-day, as first of old.
Thine the fresh song and wakened hum;
Thine the glad rill's recovered flow,
And thine the stir the sod below.
    Thy rap and tap and summons bold
    Startle the earth from slumber's hold.

O month content! My heart to thee!
No clamor now, no sudden throe—
The earth is roused; her soul is free;
How calm art thou, thy victory won,
How restful, in the restful sun!

The maiden April cometh slow,
Thou 'lt greet her like a king, and go.

"NOW THE NOISY WINDS ARE STILL."

Now the noisy winds are still;
April 's coming up the hill!
All the spring is in her train,
Led by shining ranks of rain;
  Pit, pat, patter, clatter,
  Sudden sun, and clatter, patter!—
First the blue, and then the shower;
Bursting bud, and smiling flower;
Brooks set free with tinkling ring;
Birds too full of song to sing;
Crisp old leaves astir with pride,
Where the timid violets hide,—
All things ready with a will,—
April 's coming up the hill!

CALLING THE FLOWERS.

THE wind is shaking the old dried leaves
  That would not quit their hold;
The sun slips under the stiffened grass,
  And drives away the cold.

Child Franca carries the dinner-horn
  To summon home the men;
She raises it high for a ringing blast,
  But silent it falls again:

"The men on the hill are hungry, I know,
  They 've been working for hours and hours;
But first I will blow just as kind as I can
  To call out the sweet little flowers,—

"Blow loud for the blossoms that live in the trees,
  And low for the daisies and clover;
But as soft as I can for the violets shy,
  Yes, softly—and over and over."

A SONG OF MAY.

My heart is light with May, with May,
  My heart is light with May!
The sky is soft; the coming birds
  Are silent on their way.

The miracle of flower and fruit
  Not yet the Lord hath wrought;
But never ripened Summer-time
  So bright a day hath brought.

For there is promise in the air,
  And murmurous prophecy;
All breathless and with lifted arms,
  Stand waiting shrub and tree.

To-morrow shall the blossoms glow;
  At dawn the birds will sing;

All through the stillness deep I hear
  The rushing tide of Spring.

My heart is light with May, with May,
  My heart is light with May!
And all the more that coming birds
  Are silent on their way.

SURPRISE.

WHAT was the moon a-spying
  Out of her half-shut eye?
One of her stars went flying
  Across the broad, blue sky.

BLOSSOM-SNOW.

MARCH came one morn to the door of May,
And begged the maiden to let him stay.
"I went too soon," was his whining prayer,
"I knew not the earth could grow so fair."
So she let him in; and he promised her
He would hardly breathe and never stir.

And all day long he kept his word;
Naught from the sly old guest was heard.
Now and then he would breathe a sigh
And startle the blue-birds passing by;
Or hidden violets uncover,
Or try to blow some daisy over;
Yet, for the rest, he kept his word,—
He hardly breathed, and he never stirred,
Till the sweet May murmured: "Now, my dear,
We really do not need you here,
My flowers are frightened—don't you see?
They 'd rather be alone with me."

High overhead the blossoms hung;
Full gently had the tree-tops swung.
But now he rose in sudden wrath
And whitened all the sunny path.
"Oho!" cried he, "if I must go
I 'll turn her blossoms into snow!"

Clinging and warm, they felt the spell.
Ah, how they fluttered, floated, fell!
The air was full of eddying bloom,—
A lightsome, flowery dance of doom.
In flurried heaps at last it lay,
Or drifted silently away;
And still he shook, "Good-bye! Good-bye!"
Then vanished in the trackless sky.

The branches whispered: "Now for fruit!"
And thrilled with joy from tip to root.
May, kneeling, kissed the fragrant ground;
The air was filled with peace profound;
For all things smiled, and seemed to know
The promise of the blossom-snow.

THE CONCERT.

Such a concert, dear, as I 've had to-night!
Full of sweet sound and deep delight;
    And yet "the house" was poor;
Poor, if you count by crowded seats;
But judging only by glad heart-beats,
    'T was a splendid house, I 'm sure.

First, Baby sang as well as she could
Some sweet little notes that I understood;
And wee Kate's chirp of a laugh broke out
As Willy ran in with a merry shout;
The pussy purred on the rug in state,
And the good clock ticked: "It 's late! it 's late!"

While faint in the shadows the cricket sang,
And the kettle hummed with a plaintive twang.

That was Part First, you must know, my dear,
When only we five were there to hear;
    The fagots crackled applause;
The baby's soft little pat-a-cake
Made reckless *encores* for the music's sake,
    And "lullaby" brought us the pause.

Well, the Second Part? Ah that was fine—
Fine to the heart's core, lover mine!
For over the kettle's winsome plaint,
And the baby's breathing, sweet and faint,
And over the prattle of Will and Kate,
And the clock's impatient "Late! it 's late!"
I heard the blessedest sound of all—
A click of the latch, a step in the hall!
And "Home, sweet home" pulsed all the air
As you came calling up the stair.

ANOTHER YEAR.

OLD man with the hour-glass, halt! halt! I pray—
Don't you see you are taking my children away?
My own little babies who came long ago,
You stole them, old man with the beard white as
snow!

My beautiful babies, so bonny and bright!
Where have you carried them, far out of sight?
Oh, dimpled their cheeks were, and sunny their hair!
But I cannot find them; I 've searched everywhere.

My three-year-old toddlers, they shouted in glee;
They sported about me; they sat on my knee.
Oh, their prattle and laughter were silvery rain!
Old man, must I list for their voices in vain?

They were here; they were gone while their kisses
were warm.
I scarce knew the hour when they slipped from my
arm—

Oh! where was I looking when, peerless and sweet,
They followed the track of your echoless feet?

My brave little school-boys who ran in and out,
And lifted the air with their song and their shout:
My boys on the coldest days ever a-glow,
My dear, romping school-boys who bothered me so!

There were two of them then; and one of the two—
Ah! I never was watchful enough—followed you.
My chubby-faced darling, my kite-flying pet—
Alack! all his playthings are lying here yet.

And the other. O Time! do not take him away!
For a few precious years, I implore, let him stay.
I love him—I need him—my blessing and joy!
You have had all the rest; leave me one little boy!

He halts! He will stop! No; the fall of the sand
In the hour-glass deceived me. It seemed at a stand.
But whom have we here? Jamie! Harry! how? why,
Just as many as ever—and Time passing by?

Jamie, my bouncer, my man-boy, my pride!
Harry, my sunbeam, whatever betide—
I can hardly believe it. But surely it 's clear
My babies, my toddlers, my school-boys are here!

Move on then, O Time! I have nothing to say,
You have left me far more than you 've taken away,
And yet I would whisper a word ere you go;
You 've a year of my Harry's—the last one, you
know—

How does it rank among those that have flown?
Was it worthily used when he called it his own?
God filled it with happiness, comfort and health—
Did my darling spend rightly its Love-given wealth?

No answer in words. Yet it really did seem
That the sand sparkled lightly—the scythe sent a
gleam.
Is it answer and promise? God grant it be so,
From that silent old man with the beard white as
snow.

THE MINUET.

GRANDMA told me all about it,
Told me so I could n't doubt it,
How she danced — my Grandma danced! —
        Long ago.
How she held her pretty head,
How her dainty skirt she spread,
Turning out her little toes;
How she slowly leaned and rose —
        Long ago.

Grandma's hair was bright and sunny;
Dimpled cheeks, too — ah, how funny!
  Really quite a pretty girl,
        Long ago.
Bless her! why, she wears a cap,
Grandma does, and takes a nap
Every single day; and yet
Grandma danced the minuet
        Long ago.

Now she sits there, rocking, rocking,
Always knitting Grandpa's stocking—
  (Every girl was taught to knit
      Long ago.)
Yet her figure is so neat,
And her ways so staid and sweet,
I can almost see her now
Bending to her partner's bow,
      Long ago.

Grandma says our modern jumping,
Hopping, rushing, whirling, bumping,
  Would have shocked the gentle folk
      Long ago.
No—they moved with stately grace,
Everything in proper place,
Gliding slowly forward, then
Slowly courtseying back again,
      Long ago.

Modern ways are quite alarming,
Grandma says; but boys were charming—

Girls and boys, I mean, of course—
Long ago.
Brave but modest, grandly shy,—
She would like to have us try
Just to feel like those who met
In the graceful minuet
Long ago.

Were the minuet in fashion,
Who could fly into a passion?
All would wear the calm they wore
Long ago.
In time to come, if I, perchance,
Should tell my grandchild of *our* dance,
I should really like to say:
"We did it, dear, in some such way,
Long ago."

MOTHERLESS.

"I WISH she had not died," she said;
  The words were soft and low;
"Most little girls like me, papa,
  Have dear mammas, you know.

"There 's Lulu Hart next door. Oh, dear!
  I think it is so sweet
To have your mother nod to you
  Across the window-seat.

"And often when we 're playing games,
  Lu throws a kiss up there;
And when she rolls her hoople well,
  She knows some one will care.

"Do you think God was good to take
  My own mamma away?
For I was just a baby then—
  Papa, why don't you say?"

"Yes, yes, my child," he sobbed. "Mamma
Is very happy, dear."
His little girl sprang up, nor cared
Another word to hear.

"Why, papa, crying! Please don't cry.
Do you feel sorry, too?
Now, papa, see. I never meant
I did n't care for you.

"Poor eyes! all wet. I 'll kiss them dry.
What 's in your pocket? See.
Oh, where 's your watch? Now, wont you please
Just make it tick for me?

"It 's nice to have a dear papa;—
How big it is, and bright!
I hear it *ticky*, *ticky*, *tick!*
It 's *very* loud to-night.

"Ride me to Banbury Cross, papa!
Now don't you let me fall.

When I was littler, how I slipped!
  I could n't keep on at all.

"Oh, there 's the tea-bell! Now you 've tossed
  My hair like everything!
I 'll toss yours, too. Oho! oho!
  You look just like a king—

"For kings have crowns, you know, papa,
  And your hair 's standing straight.
I knew you 'd laugh. There, now, you 're good—
  Come, quick, and show Aunt Kate."

Aunt, at the table, glanced at one,
  Then, slyly, at the other;
She could not think what hidden thing
  Had happened to her brother.
His shining hair stood like a crown,
  His smile was warm and bright,—
"Why, John," she said, "you really seem
  Like your old self to-night."

WILLIE.

THREE-YEAR-OLD Willie, barefooted Willie,
Willie with hair in a golden-thread tangle;
Tottering Willie, self-helping Willie,
Child in whom sweetness and poverty wrangle;
Willie, whose mother toils in my kitchen;
Willie, whose father carried a hod;
Willie, whose childish disdain is bolder
Than the pride of the emperor, favored of God.

Why dost thou knock at my heart, little pauper,
Bidding me love thee, entering there,
Sitting beside little cherubs who blessed me,
Thy manner half saucy and half debonair?
With garments all tattered and soiled, little Willie,
And face all begrimed? 'T is not fitting, you know,—
Velvet and laces are fine, naughty Willie,
And poor little boys should not come to me so.

The chubby intruder, still wickedly smiling,
And ah, what a shout!—Is he laughing at *me?*
Can the rascal know even the thoughts I am thinking?—
Now rushes upon me and climbs to my knee.
And though he is silent, I hear him quite plainly—
To listening hearts how a baby can speak!—
He tells me, while laces and tatters are blending,
And his sunshiny tangles are brushing my cheek:

"I 'm a poor little fellow, with no one to teach me;
But my soul is a new one—fresh from God;
And He gave me something so brave and holy,
It never can turn to an earthly clod.
The birds never sing, 'Little Willie is ragged!'
Nor the flowers, 'He will soil us. Take him away!'
But they 're glad when I happen to look and to listen,
And the blue sky is over me night and day.

"And what if my father, with hod and trowel,
Carried and toiled the whole day long,—
Did n't he comfort my mother and love her?
Did n't he cheer her with frolic and song?

I never saw him. One bright autumn morning,
  Just three years ago, he went off to the war;
Went off to battle for you and your country,
  And then—he never came back any more.

"Nevermore labored with hod and with trowel,
  Never came back with his joke and his song.
Mother would know only working and weeping
  If I were not sunny and careless and strong.
She chides me and kisses me, beats me and blesses,
  And prays to the saints that her boy may be good;
Were she rich, she would keep me as clean as a daisy,
  Not ragged and soiled in my fresh babyhood."

Say no more, Willie! Mock me and love me!
  Into my heart enter blithesomely still.
Bright little soldier's boy, poor little worker's boy,
  Shame to the coward who uses thee ill!

THE FOOT-PRINT IN THE SNOW.

Heavy and white the cold snow lay,
As, nearing my cottage one winter day,
I saw by the porch a foot-print small,
A bare little foot-print, toes and all,
Pressed—ah, so wearily!—into the snow,
As if the wee step had been jaded and slow.
"Poor little homeless waif!" I thought;
But the fleeting sympathy came to naught—
For pity may fall from a heart that 's gay
As lightly as snow-flakes melting away;
And soon would be greeting me, strong in their charms,
Bright little faces and warm little arms.

Closing the door, in a joyous glow,
I chided the children for crowding me so—
The glad little witches! as sunny and blessed
As ever a home-coming mother caressed.
Then I caught up the youngest, unnoticed before,
My sweet little Mabel, who sat on the floor.

"Why, my darling! What is it?" I cried, in surprise;
"Barefooted!" The little one lifted her eyes;
They were brimming with tears, and her cheek, too, was wet—
"Oh, my feet hurt me so!" "What has harmed them, my pet?"
"Why, just to see how it felt, you know,
I stood with my shoes off out there in the snow."

That was all. But while fondling and making them warm—
The dear little feet that had tempted the storm—
And putting on soft little stocking and shoe,
A feeling of sudden remorse pierced me through.
That lingering foot-print! How soon I forgot
When I thought 't was a beggar-child passed by my cot!
O pale-blossomed pity that never bore fruit!—
I will pluck it away from my heart, branch and root.
Love teaches at last. Now their meaning I know—
The bare little foot-prints we see in the snow.

HOW THE NEW YEAR CAME.

THE sun was sinking out of sight.
"Bessie," said Herbert, "have you heard?
It 's really true, upon my word,
This year is going away to-night.
It 's time is up, they say, and so
At midnight it will have to go.
And right away another year
Will come along, a real New Year,
As soft as any mouse—
So soft we 'll hardly hear it creep—
Yes, come right to this very house,
While every one 's asleep!"

Now, Bessie's eyes grew wide to hear.
"Let 's keep awake," she cried, "and so
We 'll see one come and see one go—
Two years at once! How very queer?
Let 's tell the New Year it is bad,
We want the one we 've always had,

With birds and flowers and things that grow,
  And funny ice and pretty snow.
  It had my birthday, too, in May,
And yours—when was it? and you know
  How it had Fourth o' July one day,
And Christmas. Oh! it *must n't* go!"

"Ha! ha!" laughed Herbert, "what a Bess!
  This year was new when first it came.
  The next one will be just the same
As this that 's going now, I guess.
  That 's nothing. But what bothers me
  Is how the change is going to be.
  I can't see how one year can go
  And one can come at midnight, so
  All in a minute—*that 's* the bother!
I 've heard them say 'the rolling year';
  You 'd think they 'd roll on one another,
  Unless they knew just how to steer."

The speck of time 'twixt day and day
  Was close at hand. Herbert and Bess

Had won their parents' smiling "Yes,"
To watch the old year go away.
All but the children were asleep,
And years might roll, or years might creep,
For all they cared; while Bess and Bert,
Who never moved and scarcely spoke,
Watched the great clock, awake, alert,
All breathless for the coming stroke.

Soon Bessie whispered: "Nell don't care."
Nell was her doll. And Herbert said,
"The clock 's so far up overhead
It makes me wink to watch it there,
The great tall thing! Let 's look inside!"
And so its door they opened wide.

TICK-A-TICK! How loud it sounded!
Bessie's heart with wonder bounded.
How the great round thing that hung
Down the middle, swung and swung!
Tick, a-tick, a-tick, a-tick—
Dear, how loud it was and quick!

Tick-a, tick-a, tick-a, tick-a!
Surely it was growing quicker!
While the swinging thing kept on
Back and forth, and never done.

There! It 's coming! Loud and clear,
Each ringing stroke the night alarms.
Bess, screaming, hid in Herbert's arms.
"The year!" he cried, "the year! the year!"
"Where?" faltered Bessie, "which? where-'bouts?"
But still "The year!" glad Herbert shouts;
And still the steady strokes rang on
Until the banished year was gone.
"We 've seen the Old Year out—hurrah!"
"Oh! oh!" sobbed Bessie, "call mamma.
I don't like years to racket so:
It frightens me to hear 'em go!"
But Herbert kissed away her tears,
And, gently soothing all her fears,
He heard the New Year coming quick,
Tick, a-tick, a-tick, a-tick!

AT THE WINDOW.

I SIT at the window and watch her,
  With my work before me spread,
My needle flashing and foiling the light;
  She trimmeth her garden-bed.

No word do I speak to the maiden
  As she trips the garden round;
Yet questions go and answers come,
  Though not on the wings of sound.

"Look deep in the rose, my Eunice,
  And tell me what you find."
"I find a love that is sweet and warm
  Glowing for all mankind."

"Now turn to the breeze, my Eunice,
  And say what doth it bear."
"It bears in the touch of its fragrant flight
  A promise of heavenly care."

" Oh, list to the birds, sweet Eunice,
  And tell me what you hear!"
" I hear a shower of blessings fall
  On all things far and near."

No word do I speak to the maiden,
  As she trips the garden round;
Yet the questions go and the answers come
  Though not on the wings of sound.

For I know in the soul of my darling,
  Lighting her gladsome youth,
Abideth a love for the Father above
  Deep as her sweetness and truth.

I sit at the window and watch her,
  Till the quick tears gather and fall;
Then quietly turn to my sewing again,
  And wonder with joy at it all.

KITTY.

"COME, Kitty, come!" they said,—
But Kitty hesitated;
Nodding oft her pretty head
  With, "I 'm coming soon.
Father 's rowing home, I know,
I cannot think what keeps him so,"
And still she stood and waited.—
  "I 'm coming soon."

"Come, Kit!" her brothers cried;
But Kitty by the water
Still eagerly the distance eyed,
  With, "I 'm coming soon.
Why what would evening be," said she,
"Without dear father home to tea?
Without his 'Ho, my daughter!'—?
  I 'm coming soon."

"Come, Kate!" her mother called,
"The supper 's almost ready."
But Kitty in her place installed,
  Coaxed, "I 'm coming soon.
Do let me wait. He 's sure to come;
By this time father 's always home—
He rows so fast and steady;
  I 'm coming soon."

"Come, Kit!" they half implore.
The girl is softly humming;
She hardly hears them any more,—
  But "I 'm coming soon"
Is in her heart; for far from shore—
Gliding the happy waters o'er—
She sees the boat, and cries, "He 's coming!
  We 're coming soon!"

AFTER TEA.

YES, somewhere far off on the ocean,
  A lover is sailing to me—
A beautiful lover! Nurse found him
  To-night in my cup, after tea.

Whenever the cruel wind whistles,
  I 'll think of that ship on the sea,
And tremble with terror lest something
  May happen quite dreadful to me.

And then, when the moon rises softly,
  I hardly can sleep in my glee,
For I 'll know that its beautiful splendor
  Is lighting my lover to me.

But oh, if he *should* come! Why, Nursey,
  I 'd hide like a mouse. Deary me!
What nonsense it is! But you should n't
  Be finding such things in my tea.

A BIRTHDAY RHYME.

TELL me, O youth so straight and tall,
  So glad with eager thought!
Have you seen of late a bouncing boy
  Brimful of merry sport?
Brimful of merry sport is he,
  A lad of fifteen summers,
With velvet lip still smooth and fair,
  But a fist that awes all comers.

He used to laugh with unconcern
  Whene'er a school-girl met him,
Unconscious quite what wondrous power
  She 'd have in time to fret him.
He only cared for "fellows" then,
  And "ball," and "tag," and "shinny,"
And thought a chap who brushed his hair
  Was just a fop or ninny.

Somehow, I loved this bouncing boy
  Because he was my own;
I had him here a year ago,
  And know not where he 's flown.
I know not where he 's flown, and yet
  Whenever you are near—
It 's very odd!—I 'm reconciled
  Because you grow so dear.

You bear great likeness to my boy
  I think, and—strange the whim!—
There 's that in you which I have prayed
  Might come in time to him.
Then if you 'll stay, my dashing youth,
  And love me like the other,
I 'll let him go, and, clasping you,
  Be still a happy mother.

So hold me close, my bigger boy,
  My larger-hearted Harry,
With broader shoulders, older head,
  And more of life to carry;

Hold close, and whisper, heart to heart,
  Our Lord has blessed us truly,
Since every year we love so well
  And find it out so newly.

With deepened joy and prayerful love,
  All in the autumn's splendor,
I hail you, boy of mine, and give
  A welcome proud and tender.
'T is grand to take the birthdays in,
  If, while the years we 're counting,
In heart and soul, in hope and aim,
  We steadily keep mounting.

THANKSGIVING.

All their heads were bowed in prayer,—
Father's, mother's, boys' and girls',
Grandma's, grandpa's—only Nelly,
Little Nelly, shook her curls.

Little Nelly shook her curls,
Smiling, gazing, all intent,
Stared, as ever, at the sight—
Wondered what on earth it meant.

Busy fire-light, flashing bright,
Shot its frisky flamelets out;
While the ship above the clock
Gayly tossed and pitched about.

Roasted turkey, on his back,
And the chickens, side by side,
Had a perky, pompous air,
Full of jollity and pride;

Tempting pies and puddings near,
  Held their faces to the light;
While canary in his cage,
  Piped and sang with all his might.

Flowery carpet under-foot,
  Hanging basket all a-bloom,
Pearly, picture-covered wall—
  Drew the sunlight to the room.

Little Nelly felt it all,
  Felt how bright it was and fair;.
And the moment seemed so long
  That the heads were bowed in prayer.

If they only knew, she thought,
  How the room was full of play,
They would never hide their faces
  In that sober, solemn way.

Laughing, puzzled, little Nell!
  How could such a baby know

'T was the cheery, sunny gladness
  That had bowed their heads so low;

That the blithesome, happy home-life,
  Birdie singing on the wall,
And the laughing little mischief,
  Made them thank the God of all.

THERE 's a ship on the sea. It is sailing to-night,
    Sailing to-night!
And father 's aboard, and the moon is all bright,
    Shining and bright!
Dear moon! he 'll be sailing for many a night—
    Sailing from mother and me.
Oh! follow the ship with your silvery light,
    As father sails over the sea!

OLD SONGS.

Alone in the twilight tender,
  I plan the coming days,
While the supple flames are lapping
  In weird, fantastic ways;
When out of the startled darkness
  There springs a single note,—
And the first light strains of a prelude
  Slow into the silence float.
'T is mother's touch! How quietly she always enters in!
With child-like throb I listen now to hear the song begin:
"*Roy's wife of Aldivalloch!*" Ah, me! The woful shame!
And "how she cheated him" I learn with honest ire and blame.
And then a moment's silence, a fallen music-page—
And gone all thought of cruel wife and sorry lover's rage.

The shadowy parlor-walls grow wide and change to
meadows fair,
For the sweet "*Blue Bells of Scotland*" are waving
in the air.
The summer sky is over them, the fragrant breezes
blow,
But, ere they fade, the voice begins in cadence sad
and slow.
"*What's this dull town to me?*" it sings. "Ah,
what indeed," I sigh,—
For "Robin is not here" it sobs, in plaintive,
broken cry.
Poor, lonely lassie! weeping sore. My heart is with
her still,
When suddenly, in changeful mood, there comes a
martial thrill;
And now I know that through the land one burst
of fervor rings,
As "*Who 'll be king but Charlie?*" the sweet voice
faintly sings.
Ah, good it is to listen here, in flitting shadows hid!—
Till comes a silken rustle; and then with folded lid

The old piano silent stands,—and the entry's swinging light
Reveals the tall, retreating form, framed in the doorway bright.
Only a moment. Vanished now the softly-kerchiefed gown;
And once again, the firelight chasing shadows up and down,
Is all I see, as thoughtfully I lift the warm brass tongs,
And turn the embers over to the echoes of old songs.

THE NIGHTLY REST.

A FOLDING darkness hangs before the dawn,
Twin curtain with our sleep;
And when they part, with mystic, dreamy sweep,
The Day smiles in our face, and we awake,
Ready once more life's noisy ways to take
Till by sweet Night the folds again are drawn.

www.ingramcontent.com/pod-product-compliance
Lightning Source LLC
LaVergne TN
LVHW021415110826
845150LV00007B/1937

* 9 7 8 1 4 2 5 5 0 9 8 3 5 *